My Stunt Double

Poems

Travis Denton

C&R Press
Conscious & Responsible

Copyright ©2018 Travis Denton

ISBN: 978-1-936196-90-6
Library of Congress Control Number: 2018955062

C&R Press
Conscious & Responsible
crpress.org

For special discounted bulk purchases, please contact:
C&R Press sales@crpress.org
Contact info@crpress.org to book events, readings and author signings.

—For Katie & Helena, always

—For Tom Lux, "inch by hammered inch"

Acknowledgements:

Many thanks to the editors of the following journals where some of these poems first appeared:

Barrow Street: "Balloons," "Buzzed, Fragile, Morning." *The Boiler Journal*: "Achilles Realizes There Is No God," "The Spiders in My House." *Bridge Eight*: "Man, one evening," "What Beauty Gives Us," "Brother, God of Projectiles." *Cimarron Review*: "Man, one day, went to see a Madam Somebody," "Man Once Stood on His Dock." *Connotation*: "Poem to the Dying Earth," "Car Idling in Grocery Store Lot." *Five Points*: "Teulada," "Bombs Over Water." *The Enchanting Verses Literary Review*: "The light in bars then, around the holidays." *Ghost Town*: "Penumbra," "Love and the Moon," "Waking a Sleeping Limb." *Mead*: "The Body." *Poetry International*: "In the Days When There Were Many Gods," "The Body Next Door."

Special thanks to: Thomas Lux, the founder of the feast for so many; Poetry@TECH; Stuart Dischell; Cathy Allman; Gary Clark and everyone at the Vermont Studio Center; James May; Chelsea Rathburn; Stephen Dobyns, Bob Hicok and Ilya Kaminsky for their stunning light; Mary and Jim Denton. And to Katie Chaple and Helena Skylark, along with all my dears—you know who you are.

I saw nobody coming, so I went instead.
    —John Berryman from "Dreamsong 76"

      Any idiot can face a crisis; it is this
      day-to-day living that wears you out.
            —often attributed to Anton Chekov

Contents

My Stunt Double

What Beauty Gives Us

When I look up at the red dot in the sky
Grazing left on the elliptical,
A dot among dots among flecks—
Concentric, gathered, lit from the dead
Lamps of the light of other days,
All I can think of is TV news
And a rover tracking its way,
Making ruts—its slow wheels climb
Dust and ice dunes as it searches
For life I cannot know—
Something with twelve arms,
A row of eyes around what we'd call
A head, I think of its dying,
Of all their dyings—how they could have died
One by one, generations—fathers, sons,
Idiots and bastards—until the very last
Stands looking out on a greeny-blue dot
Out of reach, yet he reaches, grabs for it,
Each of those arms hurling and knotting
With the others, twisting until he's tight
In a straight-jacket of arms,
Having looked up to find he's the last
Standing—the last trudging prince
Around the plain, the one to see
The light yellow and thin.
He looks out to that green dot
And not having the words, and strung up
In that weird hug, looks out to that green,
Not knowing the word
For *chapel*, or *mayday*, kneels,
But won't lie down.

S

The Body

The orange pines
For your tongue—
Starves without you.
The dance wants
Your arms and legs
Wrapped around it,
Your face nuzzled
In its neck.
The coat is empty.
Shirts, locked
Themselves away
In darkness,
Given themselves
To the hanger,
Which has given
Itself to the rack.
The moths, which ate
Your sweaters
Have chewed holes
In their wings.
Your footprints
Chase after you
And have found
Only your shoes
By a river.
And when you speak,
If you do,
Our ears
Are empty sails.

Balloons

Reported at the city's edge:
A woman on the seventy-seventh floor
Slumped over her desk looked out
To catch one hovering at her glass, then gone—
An omen of luck.
Some with notes, others with prizes or trinkets.
Early onlookers called the first
Of them messages in bottles.
People left their work:
Drinkers rushed from their barstools,
Shoppers from racks to see.
A meter maid dropped her ticket book
To beat the postman who believed
He had charge of this sort of mail.
At first they were spots in clouds,
Until traffic stopped.
Hipsters threw down their bikes.
Tokyo, Milwaukee, Calgary
And all points between reported
The sky opening, as if scored, and bled rainbow—
An unrelenting rainbow that swelled
And bellowed more rainbow.
A few clowns here and there
Pulled, twisted, and knotted them,
Tried to work them into poodle with bone,
Long sword or crown, but baffled at the shapes,
Which floated from their hands.
The slow motion fall continued into evening.
People hurried from their houses
With hatpins, kitchen knives and forks to poke at the sky.
Each balloon pregnant with fortune and wish—
A currency of horoscope and salutation.
By day's end, houses emptied, tenement and brownstone
Abandoned with the streets full of goodwill,
Everyone past questioning the source,

But shaking hands, clawing their way,
Trampling over the other,
To shake hands, congratulate, inform,
To repair a bygone rift, to make right,
To give thanks and to sing.

My Stunt Double

is running
Into a burning shotgun house in Cabbagetown.
Smoke licks his neck, cinders
Glow before him like possibility.
His footprints spark behind him
While I sit desk-side, coffee mug ring
Coalescing on a stack of forms
That need signed, but he wasn't there
When at sixteen I took a summer job
In a foundry that made bronze statues—
Eagle and Snake; Cowboy; Navajo with Eagle;
Navajo with Tear—I did it because the rest
Of my band worked there—bass player on patina,
Lead guitar on casting, and me sandblasting slurry
From the just-cooled forms—lava
Still warm as an inner thigh.
My stunt double wasn't there to see me
In full space suit, piped-in air, to watch
Through the sand-pitted shield
My hands move in the over-sized leather
Gloves—light crystalized as it spun
Through a high window.
He was just busting through
A cloud, his chute blossoming yellow in re-entry.
I wore those gloves because they said
The sandblast could strip my hand to bone
In under two seconds—
And I needed my hands for the work.
In my rock-n-roll days, my stunt double
Was called in to sweet-talk girls
After a show. I watched
The tangle of hair and hands knit
Into a good story. My job was to blast
The plaster from the art,
While the smell of my own breath and sweat

Made me sick, balancing on two feet
Of shifting sand as tablesful of work
Stared me down. I quit the job and the band,
Left Eddie, Tommy, Habeeb the Hammer
To their cast, melt, and pour, each of them
Chalked in slurry, still moving
Under the corrugated tin-framed building,
Each cooking up their next solo, left them
Looking for another drummer.
I walked out, beside me, my Double—
Hungover for six straight days,
Cigarette dangling from his lips—
Dodged a Plymouth and ran back
Into a life I still do not know.

Achilles Realizes There Is No God

Do not think of Achilles staggering—
That storied heel and poison arrow.
But think of him lying under whatever sky you can imagine,
Under whatever constellations a hero of his stature
Lies under that gets him contemplating lofty things—
Not thinking of his own unmaking, but of Patroclus,
Put down, his lover, in borrowed armor, brought low,
Arms, legs; cock and balls like sullied prunes,
And from there, that one grief,
How he ponders everyone's unmaking—
No one left standing, no planet turning,
Every camp and city fallen—
Tents left to cinder, kicked-in doors, walls down,
Hector cut down.
But what's more than that single grief—
Set in the old-time story of loss and revenge,
Achilles grows lonely to understand
He's even unmade the gods who made him,
That not a goddamned thing is wrought or destined,
Something the least of us find—
No divine mover, all moving in retrograde or rusting,
And from then on he sees only fire, nothing but fire.

Dear Seventeen-Year Cicadas:

As you pitch and yaw under a foot of dirt,
Nearly two decades like a single night
And with dawn rounding the hemisphere
As you wiggle toward moon or sun—
Toward whatever primal thing calls you—something
My body has forgotten—call it urge, instinct,
Divine mover, something in the gut,
Do you remember your jaws full of marigold,
Wind gusting to the east way back in 1999,
When you and your billions felt a churn
Toward the mortal, dove and burrowed,
Not like a thing with wings,
But like those who know more
Of death than any creature? As you clawed,
Spit sand, I saw rising everywhere:
Leaves fell back to branches, fog bloomed
Then rose, never just burned away—
Buildings went up all over.

Buzzed, Fragile, Morning

I was buzzed this morning
On champagne and juice,
Over eggs and caffeine,
Not some brunch thing,
Pouring the news over
The table like molasses,
Singing about the West Coast
With its canyons and big sky,
Its stars and happenings,
And about that time,
A dove perched
On the back of your chair,
Calling out like the newly born
Met with first breath,
And it was like all that's been
Undone was made whole
Like my mother's birds,
Doves, too, I think, swept off
A shelf by boys'
Curiosity, made Humpty Dumpty
Whole, with glue and thinned paint,
And as she lifted them
To a higher ledge,
I swear to you,
They flew from her hand.

What the Satellite Saw

Floating on a wave of anti-gravity, it beams
A cloud six-hundred miles across
With an eye staring back into space,
Unearthly Cyclops. The ocean

Has crawled back from the beach,
Boats ebb on a sandy pudding,
And the rain falls sideways.
Amid boil warnings, we stew

Our nouns and verbs into simple sentences
By candlelight. If this is the apocalypse
And the zombies toddle out near dusk,
We'll be there like empty grocery store shelves,

Canned goods burrowed out the sliding doors,
Our hearts like batteries. We brush our teeth
In bottled water as the water on the street rises,
And the storm surge in all of us

In all its holy ghostiness pronounces us alive
As we Google what to make with the hail
The storm left—ice cream? Or if it's enough
We'll pack our wounds with it.

Praise the dark—the street lights out,
The moon out, no planes overhead,
No sirens, dog walkers kenneled
For the day, whole cities sparking

As lines go down, and you roll over,
Touch my face and remind me,
Happy apocalypse, baby,
Happy apocalypse, this is all we get.

In the Days When There Were Many Gods

There was a barn owl with an arrow through one eye
That lived in my back yard—at any second it was staring
Down the shaft of the weapon with its one good eye—
The feathered end of the bolt sticking from the back of its head.
At that moment in my life between grad school and watching
Another woman pack her car, and with the thrill
Of a quiet house and its empty bed, I stood ready to praise,
Once again, the sirens on the street, and windows vibrating
Near dawn with the first bus headed downtown.
I was still amazed at the many gods there were in the world then—
Their watchful eyes waiting to feed some hunger
To punish or promote. I'd sit on the back patio with red wine,
My favorite of the punisher gods, and the tenacious sense
Of consequence that said everything I did meant something,
And I'd watch the bird. I thought of the opossum that lived
Under the shed and pictured it lumbering out past dark
And pitting his spikes of teeth against the owl's tines.
And having exhausted all the others, I'd pray
To that raptor, god of the blood moon, and new moon,
God of the survivor, god of the last one standing, god of the slow
To wrath, god of the oak tree in my back yard, god
Of the North American Marsupial. Some days
I'd sit there, the owl ten feet above me
In his oaky perch and watch it watch
My terrier chase tennis balls—the owl's head
Like a surveillance camera tracking its every move, or staring
Into the middle distance of Atlanta's skyline—the arrow
In the owl's eye like a compass pointing north, northwest, due south.

Donor

His chest—that little cage rattles with absence,
A face he can't quite put together,
Never enough pieces when he tries.
There's a city in blackout there, theaters gone dark
With players reading their lines by flashlight.
He misses his heart—that flow and bilge
He measured in seconds flatlines into memory.
Arms? He only sees them out
His study window in a pine.
His feet, he won't talk about—turns away
As they pass him on a sidewalk, in the grocery,
Out in the evening, near the lake.
They're a puzzle of sinew and bone,
The left, a smooth gait; the other,
Always a step behind, untrue like a busted cog.
All of it, gone—his legs tread along,
Rewriting the story of water.
Standing just there, where was it that he went?
He puzzles now, with all of him gifted,
Yet he remembers more of love than anyone,
Even with every joint, scar, or length of spine
Only ghost pain or pleasure now.
His eyes: he can't place the color,
Couldn't pick them out in a line-up;
The broken whistle of his mouth, he let that go too,
And his voice, wherever it is, just some tune
He'll chase around all night.

Brother: God of Projectiles

He was good with them, anything
Thrown or launched, with ragged edge,
Fuse—a superpower all his own.
Take softball, the mere calling out of my name,
Travis, like an incantation,
His fingers already knuckled
Around the ball, *Travis*,
And with a twist, I turned and the ball
Rounded me in the forehead—
The azaleas spun into magenta spheres
Dangling along the solar plain as the front yard went dark.
I still have a knot and damage to the frontal lobe,
Causing trouble with simple decisions,
Problems with night vision and perspective.
There was the hickory nut incident, my name called,
As if it was the first time I'd heard it shouted
Across the yard *I'm here*, then, hickory nut to the jaw,
Stitches and Brother squawking at his fine shot—
A death blow in most comics.
And later, Independence Day, my name again,
Travis, over the blare of Tom Petty from the car,
Travis, and I turned to a handful of bottle rockets,
And a braided fuse that would burn
Through my middle years to now—
Travis, but they'd not launch, not fly, not go forth,
Not kvetch like some mortar
Climbing out of the beach at Normandy,
But him clutching the fire too tight,
Gauging it all wrong, holding on,
The fire blossoming in his hands
Like daylilies, then hiss and bang.
And to think, I remember this now,
Pissing off the deck of this rented cabin, into the red palm
Of a giant maple leaf twenty feet below,
The snap of a hardwood fire behind me, *Travis*.

The Body Next Door

Our neighbor hasn't been spotted
For weeks, at least by us—84 years old,
Pencil moustache, gray fedora. His cars
Haven't moved, tan Lincoln pointed

Toward the street, poised for a get-away,
Yet one back tire, flat like a rubber chicken.
We watch his windows at night for motion—
No lights, only a sewer rat pushing through the blinds

Like a fist. My wife suspects he's in there,
In the threshold to the kitchen, arms stretched
Out for the phone inches from his fingers,
Face and eyes caught in that look of wonder

That only the dead have perfected. The sun will
Rise, set—rooms brighten, go dark. On a Sunday,
Late August, unusual for flies in Atlanta, but
When the air is thick with them, "Who should we call?"

She asks. Getting back from dinner
And the stench of rotting potatoes has settled
On our porch—"Should we knock?"
His mail is piling up. Front porch light, out.

I've begun to imagine him,
Not facedown on checkered linoleum,
But having wandered off toward the woods
One evening, losing a slipper on a tree stump,

Limping into that forest, his ex-wives asleep
Elsewhere. He's forgotten the word for "rescue,"
His past, just a smudge. He mistakes
A truck on the nearby interstate for a helicopter,

Looks up through the canopy of leaves
Like church windows.
We hear his phone most nights,
Like a fire alarm, it shouts its way

Toward the exits, but no one jerks the brass knobs,
Throws open the doors and runs across
His knee-high lawn, making it to the street.

The light in bars then, around the holidays

Was always like the end of some film—
Any film—where the protagonist got nearly all
He wanted, left the rest to waste.
The camera pulls in close, catches

A drag of a cigarette, pans to ashtray
And snuffed fire, then to lights
Strung behind the glasses—a new year
Leans in to take stock of his silence

Which spills out the doors, into the street
And makes a joyful noise, like the sound
Of someone's leaving town for good. Each time
I see that, I'm back in a bar in Cabbagetown,

Near Christmas, in another life, I like to say,
Because it is not my life now. My occasional
Drinking pal Navajo Herb (still alive
And gloriously drunk), Vietnam vet and assassin

From a secret army unit—his ragged copy of the *I-Ching*
Spread before him, Black Russian sweating in his left hand.
I tell him (and remember what I said exactly,
Though not why I said it),

Herb, what's the point of light
You have to strike a match to find?
Travis, your heart is not an empty room.
Herb, what became of the breath of those you put down?

Travis, you are not the doer, but the instrument of the doer.
And with that, his car just outside—
The moon kneeling, knowing it's always later
Than anyone thinks—the city was a cathedral,
Such a serious house, its streets, the stretch between pews.

Man, one day, went to see a Madam Somebody,

a woman who lived in a white house on an embankment on the town bypass, which used to be Main Street. The woman sold answers, and he was prepared to be grateful. She pointed him to a couch, and he was stricken—where did she keep the crystal ball, the sacred heart candles, or beaded curtain? This place was just like his own life, his own house, surely if he took the aging woman to her bed, it would feel like his own bed, she, like his own wife, but he stayed. He liked the way the house smelled of shoe leather and matches, which reminded him of sliding across the plank floor on his back under his grandparents' bed and with voices creaking into cane chairs on the porch. He'd struck matches, held them to the linen cloth that covered the batting strips of the bed frame, watched as the thread went into the air—from linen to glowing strip, to air. The man thought of a childhood of struck matches tossed in a creek near the house. The woman placed her hand on his, and he realized he'd told her the story, spared no detail or fact. He told her his troubles: his wife wouldn't look at him as they made love, and he took that to mean she was thinking of another. His lawn would not grow as did other men's lawns on his block. He was there to find something he thought he'd lost. The woman smiled. When he felt himself thinking too kindly of the Madam, he told her that he'd come to her for answers. He told her that each time he walked up to a counter at a store or station to fill up, or bar, he shoved his hands into his pockets, sure that he had silver coin enough to pay, but pulled out handfuls of only pennies and plug nickels. The woman told him to take his phone to a deep lake, rent a boat and row to the center and drop his phone and watch it until the screen went dark and imagine that phone there at the bottom, its screen stark and like a sentinel in the murk, a beacon going on, its ring drowned by the current's wash and tug. He did this and fell back into the tracks of his days, kicked onward like a kid on a tricycle. But as he pressed along, he thought of the woman and the phone: the way she'd looked at him, and he understood like a scout set loose in the woods and late for dinner, but remembering the compass in his pocket. He thought of all the missed calls and messages buzzing into the dark, and mystery returned—the unseen made real as a clean window. His grass grew. One day the man had a child who grew to be bright and athletic. And they were happy all the days of their lives. When he rocked the child or pushed him in a swing, he thought of the old Madam and the white house that stood on the embankment on the town bypass, which used to be Main Street.

Born to Run

*At night we ride through the mansions of glory in suicide machines
Spring from cages out on Highway 9...*
—Bruce Springsteen

Nothing else was real then—the world,
All it was and would ever be, stuffed
In 26 volumes of encyclopedia—the presidents,
Only as real as Johnny Cash who spun
Like a spool of denim thread
Through an 8-track in my father's
Green Chrysler. New York, Madonna,
All logged, photographed, stationed in a magazine
On the living room coffee table. It was all
Saturday night and the washing of cars ritual,
Shirtless, Cedartown, Georgia, and my brother's
Souped up Mazda, before water restrictions,
Vaseline shimmer on the dash.
We sponged the chrome wheels,
Crunched newsprint on the windshield
Sopping Windex. Even my father's bronze
Stars from Vietnam, his dress blues and fatigues—
Just framed or boxed—the paintings
He brought back, just props for a story—big talk
Of mortar shells and returned fire. I tried
To picture him, a bullet in his shoulder,
Scampering under barbed wire, tried
To hear the dying, the blood-soaked men
In brown, the sky lit up with bombs,
Wanted to walk the burned-out villages,
But all I got was grass crunching under foot,
Homework, a soapy sponge, a push mower,
And this man returned from far afield in knee shorts
And a white T, a killer, spraying a beach
In machine gun muzzle flash, and Springsteen
Belting from the car, gas fumes, all four doors open.

Searching for Amelia Earhart

I'm having trouble picturing you anywhere now—
I spent good years thinking of 1937, you and Fred
Over the Pacific, blown off course and low

On fuel, locked in each other's gaze, holding
Hands over the throttle, your engines cut,
Just breeze where there should have been roar, laughter.

How many times you must have pictured that quiet
Sitting out with a drink watching the sky?
I've pictured you buckled in at 17,000 feet

Down, the high cheek bones under your freckles.
But there are many theories now—surgically ditching
Into an atoll, your blind S-O-S, voice calm,

Until days later, the Electra slips into high tide, leaving
You and Fred over a signal fire, comparing its light
To the moon—another rescue plane close,

But pitching back toward land. And the yarn
About you picked up by the Japanese—there's a grainy photo
Excavated from some archive with you staring out to sea,

The Electra on a barge, Fred talking his way out of it,
But you both die in a prison in Saipan. Amelia,
Wherever you are, I thought of you when the doctor

Looked up from my father who's forgotten how to swallow,
Like it was a set of keys to his truck left on a dresser,
Like keys, Amelia, mislaid in a barn on a high shelf—

And the doctor repeats "could be dementia;" I look
My father in the eyes, and wonder where he is
In all this, because, fuck it, Amelia, I'm lost.

We knew we were lucky

                         driving away
In my friend's blue Beetle, gears grinding
Down Lavender Mountain, curling between ditches
And overgrowth we knew was out
Of our headlights' reach. We knew we were lucky
As we gritted our teeth with each pothole, and I held on
To the dash, letting go long enough to turn off
The blasting radio, leaving just engine sputter,
And gravel chew under wheel. My friend put up
His window to make the wind stop.
                             And to think,
We knew we were lucky minutes earlier when we pulled up
To the peak and got out to smoke
Cigarettes and follow the lines of street lights below
Along the confluence of the three rivers, lucky to see
The Milky Way above us and finally something to wish on.
Exploding into a full run, we knew we were lucky
To be free, arms pumping, carrying
Us away from the spot where my then-girlfriend
Fell—disappeared below the high beams,
Into a pool of dark, and my friend shined
His light on her body spread over a dead calf—
Its throat opened, legs tied from some ritual.
Her arms flailing, mouth moving like someone blaring
Forth a new truth, but I didn't hear anything, even the cicadas
Climbed back into their little deaths; tree frogs, dumbstruck.
And everyone in that scene could be a thousand miles away
Right now, or dead, and I wouldn't know or care, and the road
Up Lavender Mountain could have peeled off by now,
But how lucky to go back to that same spot exactly
Over and over again.

The Rooms We've Left or Never Entered

I imagine emptiness and all that fills it:
King Tut's tomb before its opening and curse spilling out
Like a deep breath held too long—what it was like there
Without shadow, only the scrape of stone settling,

A drip, like cannon fire in the perfect quiet.
Or my bedroom at fourteen, sealed by the weight of thirty years,
Which is equal to the lbs. of pressure surrounding the just-discovered
British sub HMS Trespasser off the coast of Sardinia, 100 meters

Down—the thing still sealed—flooded by only memory—
Captain strapped in his chair, first mate scribbling on a roll
Of toilet paper—no one ever knowing 100 meters is an entirely
Swimmable distance for a fit young man—the sun still visible

At that depth, a compass always north. And my friend says he can't
  take
The not-knowing, can't fathom at any depth his living room in the
  mountains
When no one's there, so he shows me his camera that's always on,
How it beams to his computer all that quiet—tree shadow passing

Along the kitchen. We watch a squirrel on the landing, a workman
Filching a beer from his fridge. My friend laughs in absentia, and later
We turn on the mic and take turns speaking into that space,
"Mayday, mayday," filling it like a megaphone that distorts
Into every corner and watch the sun go down a four-hour drive away.

Good-bye the Way You Imagined It Would Sound

There's always the moment when you say good-bye to a friend,
Watch the heat waves on the road close some portal behind them.
You walk back into a quieter house, though the radio drones
From the kitchen. You imagine their fingers fumbling
With the radio as they drift back into their own selves—
The part that is not your friend, in fact, has never
Met you. The part that falls asleep in an empty room
With the TV on. The part that smiles at the teller, but doesn't speak.
The part that would mistake you for a stranger
On the street if given half a chance. And just then, the way
The sun sparks a prism through your window,
It's as if you've lived surrounded on all sides by vast fields.
The cornrows straight as the life you wanted. Beyond
Each row is another row, and beyond that row are more rows,
And when the fields catch fire come spring, each row,
You know, is a fuse leading back to the place where you live.

Poem to the Dying Earth

When we heard the giant was late
In his dying years, festering,
Would be swallowing the earth,
Take us all into himself,
We were amazed, offended to think
Our ivy would vaporize in his veins,
That his eyes would bulge
With the fire of our years,
That our memories would remind him
Of first kisses and picnics,
That footsteps in dark alleys
Would remind him of bad decisions,
That our words would no longer mean,
But be thick in the sounds
Of lovemaking. And when
Our scientists interjected
In their scientific ways
That twelve years would pass
Before he'd grow wicked
And old and overwrought,
That children conceived today
Would not make teens before his fire
Put us out, many were angry
And thought of throwing themselves
Into the conflagration
While others were sorry
For the fire, how its blaze
Would flare, then wane, go dark,
And others schemed.
We were all making plans
As to what we'd do as it neared.
Around the water cooler,
Bill said he'd take the boss's wife—
We'd never heard him talk
That way, the former minister,

Father of three, loving husband.
Some went the other way,
Seeking gods who promised fire—
They ripped their button-downs,
Tore at their sleeves in alignment.
We knew the sun had faltered,
Showing its age. We watched
As Mercury flared in orbit,
Just a blip, a silent film.
TV news reported our discoveries
Of how planets die
And from that came cures
For most cancers, spinal injuries,
Mental retardation—the lame walked
And we cheered, counted days,
Hospitals emptied, wars ended,
And as the sun just nicked Venus,
We took to calling it God.
And we watched
As God got closer
And he grew fierce, until
We could see nothing but light.

Teulada

If the bougainvillea and palms,
Juniper and scorched mountain
Staring down the sky;

If the green rock outcrops
Just under the blue skin
And the gull overseeing it all;

If the distance that expands
Where the sky dips
To a single line;

If the fish could promise
That my pitching off that roadside
Pull-off guardrail like a diving board
Meant no one would later find me
Rotting like some teenage girl
Fished from a river, half-naked
Having died horribly and soon;

If anything with teeth or claws
Could promise to not spill its guts
To a fisher's hook, but take me far
Down and not stop at some ship's wreckage
Or Roman urn sifting into sand,
And take my hands, chest,
Muscle and cocoon tattoo
To where clouds crowded
Above like old men in a park
Shaking hands with the boy
Who has beaten them all at chess can't see,

I would leave this table and wine,
This song and trumpet, this good company,

This lover—all glad for me and cheering—
Right now to get back there,
My knuckles tight against
The wheel of this rented car.

Penumbra

I

We wrapped eggs in Styrofoam peanuts,
Boxed them in newsprint,
A worn t-shirt, and on Teacher's count,
Tossed them from the roof of the building
As lightly as I've come to know, too late
Entering a room where a lover is sleeping,
After my own returning
From another lover's bed—
My own heart still in that box,
Jolted at every snore and sigh,
Yet wanting
To smash a chandelier, sweep perfume
Bottles from the dresser, trip over a shoe.

II

When we painted landscapes, Teacher told us to think
How the slope of the slide on the playground
Was like the slope of the hill to the lower field.
I thought it like the slope of her breasts.
We were told to notice how sunlight slants across it all,
That we'd soon need all we could get,
To breathe it in, wish for only sun—
Caught in a many-sided shadow,
Night's dense fog baffling the exits.

III

When Teacher laid cardboard squares
On our desks, told us if we were
Careful, that, and luck would save our eyes.
We matched her folds exactly
Because our sight depended on it,

Ripped duct tape like picking scabs.
But for the next 7.5 minutes we'd practice
The light dimming, the night coming, going.
We stepped into the eclipse
Single file—the moon and sun
Aligned in syzygy—told if we looked up
Our retinas would burn out,
Cause sparks in our brains,
And our mothers' faces would be the first to go,
The soft blue of the sky would always be beyond us,
Our siblings, a thump to the cheek.
As it went dark, the sun wreathed in a purple bruise,
We pulled on our helmets, looked out
Through a dot which let in a pin-sized ray,
That resembled, as we were instructed,
All we'd come to know of grace.

A Near Always, and Then

I

Some will be sorry to hear that tonight

After you count the steps to your room
And the lights in your house collapse,

Exhausted, into the storied dark,
And you lay down, your robe cinched

Around you like a gun belt,
Six shooters at your sides,

Your walls will dissolve
Into the corners of the house,

Your windows shudder under the weight of it all.
Your books will rewrite all their own endings,

Mosquitos carry off your lawn chairs,
Your car pushes itself out of the drive.

There's a woman who sleeps beside you,
Who will shake her head when the officers come,

Tell them that the wild horse that grazed
Inside you carried you off,

That, maybe, she saw your slippers tip-toe
Out of the house and you followed

And were caught in the wake
Of a moon one wears like a heavy coat.

II

When one is caught out

Having followed his shoes only steps
From his home to find he has crossed hills,

Spanned cities, a river, and lost the trail,
His satchel, full of what he's found,

If only a little worn—he does not look
Back for his porch light hazing yellow

Or the woman at his door with the men
Who have come to question her.

He scans for a marker, not a beacon
Like a speck on a dark movie screen,

Or a crowd gathering,
But finds something like a meadow,

One blazed in orange blooms,
A sorrow of clouds over it all, and it rolls out

Like a jazz band, the sax steering them on,
Head, melody, solo, repeat, repeat.

It's almost like that, now that he's lost,
Scaled off the map and found

This meadow that goes on.
He keeps high-stepping

The grass, until he comes to a precipice,
And he is there more fully

Than anywhere he's ever been.
There may be a yarn

Of river below, but across
The channel, washed out,

Almost formed
                    is a near always, and then.

Letter to Those Who Prophesied My Doom
(a fragment)

When you wake, you will find yourself
In a wasp nest—the walls draped with buzzing
Wings painted like cathedral windows.

Your dinner will crunch
With the broken bottles of your youth.

When you pass a mirror,
It will not recognize you.

When you pray, god will raise a hand
To signal you stop interrupting.

When you take off your hat,
Your head will come with it, and you will
Leave it on a hook in a hall you won't remember.

Where We Left Off

You were squeezing the toothpaste
Like you were killing it—
You somehow wanting to peel
Back the calendar to the Monday night
Before last, when our neighbor
A block over was gunned down.
His brother knew to tell him
A story as he bled out.
We heard the shot, yet not knowing
It was a shot, you slammed
The door as answer, joked
About champagne corks, and cheered.
Maybe I was waiting for you to end
Your sentence that rattled on
Like the jagged teeth of Atlanta's skyline.
I remember trying to answer you in Spanish,
But lost you to a verb ending,
Proper nouns chewed off.
No matter, my Pagan
With your slow moon and tides,
Dear—it never gets dark here anymore—
Maybe that's why we're not sleeping.

Car Idling in Grocery Store Lot

No broken door pulls or lost radio knobs—
No torn leather, expired insurance.
We were not homeless.
And it was not that we were trudging West
To skirt an ex-lover and tax debt.
As I remember, the other cars weren't rolling
Through the lot, but drifting along,
As priests do when their hands are full
Of ash and blessings. Looking up,
There was no trace of our bodies
In the constellations, which you took to mean
We were never "here." Imagine that: never here
Drinking gin to come down
From too much caffeine,
Never here—our patent leather hearts,
With no strings, but buckles and diamonds,
Squarely in their chests. Never here,
Too far from the interstate for a strip club,
All night buffet, or lot lizards
Tapping our driver-side glass.
You lay your car seat back,
Thought again of constellations and found
Two fish swimming in the space between
Saturn's rings—in that infinite, concentric wide open
Like the Old West to which we were headed,
But aloft, strung up in that dark matter,
Where those bodies careen dark corners,
Mounting the back turns, skidding away
To a place so distant you thought
You saw my waving back.

Post Apocalypse

He opened a book, and saw his own face
On every page, his name
Scrawled between the margins.
He thought how the world had become dangerous
In that afternoon. Random bombings in far-off places,
Earthquakes, disease once kept him up nights,
But now his chest was papier-mâché,
His back, a canvas. In years to come,
He'd yellow like newsprint,
Crack, spot with mold spores; there'd be oxidation,
Cellulose breakdown—his body,
A folio, a Gutenberg. He couldn't say if *all*
Was like him now. He shuddered to look out
The window (so he didn't) and see
The world's own change: his lawn
Like gift wrap, his street—cardboard, and the sky
Endless reams of high cotton—planes twisting,
Confetti contrails swirling behind them,
Origami birds keening, and agile as ever,
That everything known, every metaphor was to be re-trained—
And the universe—no longer a giant clock,
But strung up in a mobile, like over a crib,
Turning in its own time. And God, who let this happen,
Full of His own great revision, changed too—
Now, an encyclopedia, annotated history,
A long story caught in the crossed arms of a book.

Frank Hayes

Jockey Hayes dropped dead from his saddle
after riding Miss A. M. Frayling's jumper
Sweet Kiss to a splendid victory...
            —New York Times, June 5, 1923

When your heart gave out
And you spent your last rush,
You were pulling out front,
Twenty jock-ied horses tailing you,

That last breath mingling with track dust,
A blooming cosmos of smoke screen,

Ten thousand people looking on festooned
In Sunday clothes and hats. A fat man
Barked his 20-to-1 windfall, bought the house
A round, as you, the dark horse, Frank, stretched on.

Sweet Kiss, your bay mare, caught that bridle tug,
Veered, grazed another rider rounding

The last turn as your legs went limp
In the stirrups, riding crop tucked, head down,
Slack-jawed, your heart pattering
A few seconds more like a faucet gone to drip.

I imagine those hooves pounding under you,
Square in your saddle—sunlight on your racing silks

At just the right angle where it feels like grace—
Belmont Park on its feet for you, Frank—
Stable boy to Guinness Record, first
Dead man to win a steeplechase.

First wins are like that—
Like first kisses, which are like jumping off

A bridge into cold water, your pals
Egging you on, then splash,
Sinking as far as you can, until silt
Squishes between your toes,

And you look up at the crazed skin of water,
And wonder if you'll ever get your breath again.

And, Etc.

What you strain to get at are past
Lovers—that's why you're here,
(In this almost-familiar room

You've fashioned from memory
With shag carpet and brocade curtains,
Boxes marked 1990, and, etc.,)—

Yet when you stumble down the list,
And their faces come to you or don't,
You drift into the sweet, old etc.,

Where you left this arm and that clavicle,
This mouth, that thigh, femur,
Piled at the edge of the field

Near the house where you live now,
And you walk there nights, or as close as you can
Before you leave them to their husbands,

Mortgage, pensions, their own small deaths,
And the cold of distance drives you back
Toward the porch light, all else, etc.

Man once thought himself

Not unlike most other men: he cut the grass
When it grew, weaving the trimmer
Around the rose bushes and lilies.
He went to work each day,
Packing his lunch in a sack, then packing the sack
In his briefcase, then tucking his briefcase in his trunk.
When the weather changed, he watched his roses change,
Raked leaves from his lawn, picked up sticks
And put them at the road for someone else to collect.
He went to work. He came home.
One night this man found himself in bed
Like each night before, but this night
The bed covers knotted in his hand,
He sighed a long sigh, one that's meant to alert,
Or wake another. *That fucking dog, I'll show him.*
He thought of punching his neighbor's
Door until the lights came on.
But he realized there was no barking dog.
The street was silent, and his wife
Was not snoring her usual snore. It was quiet
And he cursed the silence,
Wished he could take it up in his hands,
Wrap his hands around that soft body.
He'd pitch that shadow from the moving train
Of his bed and be thought hero by all.
He thought of moving to the sofa,
Of trying out the quiet in another room, or taking his pillow
To the porch swing. He thought of taking his own body
Out of its skin and putting on the skin of that silence
And sloaking about the neighborhood, throwing rocks at dogs,
Peeking in windows, but he was afraid
That all he'd find were houses, all of them

With men like him twisting their covers into knots,
Damning the silence and considering other rooms,
All knowing that a tap at the window
Or police car rushing to a call would go unheard.

Homo Erectus

Mid-sentence, the morning after
Vermont snow, your left foot
Slid ahead of you, arms out to either side,

Where vultures would have thought you
A scarecrow and spiraled north.
Your locution, congealed to growl,

All guttural—caveman speak, mid the notion
Of impact, and sprawling on the concrete
Like a suicide, a body like ticker tape, the world slowing

Like glassblower's breath,
Green Mountains listing out of view.
But, the body corrects—

In that strange dance, a twitch in the calf,
Metatarsal clinch, the head tilts, shoulders row
The air—the exact equation of it all,

Shelved in the brain—knotted into double helix—
Seven million years of fine tuning—digging,
Cutting stone, comes to a clavicle, pelvic bone,

Bit of chin found at the bottom of a hole in Africa,
And you, here, biped, recovered, upright.

The Way Back

The medics pull the needle from your chest,
Slide their syringes into their sleeves.
The ambulance backs up to the scene
And lifts you from the back, placing your body
In the driver's seat—belt tight around you.
Your crushed ankle, that constellation,
Its particles adrift, is like the Big Bang
Calling back its myriad rock, its gravity, fire.
Two towns over, someone puts down the phone,
It rings as she levels back on the couch,
Wondering if it's cop show or game night.
The busted fenders heal; antifreeze
Drips up into its reservoir.
The windshield un-crazes, and you think
You see a satellite trail through
Tree sap and road dirt.
The girl who hit you wakes,
The steering wheel having blossomed
Like a poinsettia from her torso
As her headlights dim around a curve.
Your pulse, regular now as a tin drum.
The radio statics to crescendo, sputters
To verse as you back away
And you're driving, just driving back
To a birthday party, cars pass,
Brake lights in rearview.
You burst with song.

Saturday with Plymouth Duster

Our gold Duster jacked up
On two wheels, only my father's legs
Jutted from under the chrome like someone
In the throes of a suicide—his feet jerking

As he torqued a wrench in between his breathy
Dammit, fuck me, balls—army words
He wore like fatigues. I still see his hands
Coming at me as I called out after finding a razor blade

In his toolbox, and at six, watched a red blossom
Rise out of my left pointer when I sliced
Through nerve and landed bone. His hands gelled
In axle grease and up to his elbows in brake dust,

He grabbed my arms, shook me as the crime scene
Expanded with blood splatter. He was roughly
The age then as I am now. I imagine him pushing
His way from under the engine—the one thing

He knew for sure, could predict like a sunrise:
The rhythm of piston and crank shaft,
The flight of fuel to carburetor to exhaust,
Not bleeding boys with their mothers somewhere

Between town and home. We stood there,
Both of us, his filthy hands holding mine up to the light.

Bombs over Water

You pour the prosecco, add juice.
We click our glasses, they chime,
And we salute the sliding doors,
Potatoes, La Medusa—the glassy Mediterranean,
Romans, and all things we cannot control.
We sip, and just over the bay are bombs,
Just as the landlord warned—
Percussive, satisfying, then another—
Sound burst into breath of orange dust, exhaled.
The ocean sprays the rocks, but further
From our clay tile, rocks spray rocks,
Dust sprays the sky, seen miles away in the town
Where a local man unbuttons his uniform and thanks
The cloud, which thanks the dust, which thanks the rock,
Which thanks the ground, which thanks the bomb.
Another blast, and we feel our drinks,
Make jokes about getting bombed—
Thankful for distance.
As we imagine bombs getting closer,
We yell over sirens,
Roar of tank and engine—toast our last
Minutes together, embrace,
Say things we pretend not to mean,
Yet glad to be here, on this Italian island,
In this villa, where gulls screech between blasts
And wind slams doors; you duck and cover
While red dust powders the palms.

Love Letter to My Failed Crisis

You were right there like a word on the tip of the tongue.
The horizon set to go dark, the Enola Gay sailing
Over the Pacific, mushroom cloud tucked
Like a child in bed waiting to blossom. Your titanic
Beauty simmering like a frozen continent.
My Hale-Bopp comet of the heart—my tropical punch
Kool-Aid as the big guns kick in the door.

Oh, my glorious Bay of Pigs—
No matter where you ended up, whatever dumpster
You're hiding in today in Omaha, or disguised
In a cap and Hawaiian print shirt along a parade route,
I want you to know now, I'd trade this *everyday* for you—
This grinding down, this slow waking, for your sudden quake—
Tether-snap above the tram—that instant when we know
We "should have" or "wish we never did," that moment
When the medic reaches for a wrist, lifts it like a lover's
In one hand, eyes the traffic on the street, the forest of legs
Gathered near him like a playground scuffle, and then, nothing.

Man Sits on Bench Beside Lake

Each time man stares into murky dark
Of page, gazes through syllable,
Slick diphthong of tide and wave,
Man does not think of Woman home,
How Woman must be sliding key in lock,
Knob clicking, car engine clicking too, as it cools,
Or how Woman enters kitchen and jumps
As Woman's shadow takes the shape of Man
Moving faster than Woman can pull away.

Instead, Man thinks of Fish underneath,
Making Fish's way deeper to sunken tire, sneaker,
Then rising, chasing some bubble and not at all
Thinking *hunger* until Fish spots crumb
In middle distance, and mistaking opportunity
For hunger, again, slams the crust
To the roof of Fish's mouth and not thinking
Son-of-a-bitch or bloody gill,
Or Kid clapping and awing at prism of scale
Flicking off and crazing in light—
Fish only knows flight, jerk, and wriggle,
Can't know red, orange, and blue inside Fish
And how beautiful and worthless they are
And how if he had arms, and all day,
He could not hold that inside in or take it back.

On the elevator

you nodded my way,
The feet ticking above us like the week before—
You in such a nice yellow dress,
Cut just above your knee.
We dropped stories, imagined the cave walls outside,
The petroglyphs that must have papered them,
The perfect light dimming
To unflinching dark with each moment,
And stopping, not a small jolt or budge,
The canary in your pocket spoke,
Just to prove something about tomorrows.
I lit a cigarette, passed it your way
And we gave thanks for the smoke
And my bruised knuckles
And for the crow's feet stammering around our eyes.
The doors opened, you took my hand,
Stepped out, the air was cool
And the canary sang like a clock
Until he was breathless.

Man one night sitting out with a drink

Remembered himself
A young musician, a thousand miles
From leash or tether, spread out
On a leather sofa in a third-floor bar
On Avenue A with a girl
Watching the *Magnificent Seven*
Projected with no sound on a building
Across the street—Brynner, Bronson, McQueen,
All miming the words at him, *Do it, son,* and he did.
He took the girl's hand. McQueen yelled,
Kiss her, and he slugged his rusty nail,
Grabbed the back of her neck
And kissed this girl who played
At novels and piano. She went along
Then pulled back, and he could
Not hear her over the music,
But watched her mouth something like, Again, please.
He did, and she did not stop him.
Man looked over her shoulder
At the gunslingers on horseback
Across the street firing off warning shots.
Bronson, called out, *Take her home,* and he did.
They lay in the city's undark, her roommate,
A Russian dealer named Yevgeny in the kitchen,
Sacked out, already more than a day in a cocoon
Of four grams and rice wine—
The pair, taking turns getting up
In the night to bang his chest
When his snoring stopped too long. They lay there
In her twin bed, and he did not think
Of one back South who'd leave all
She thought he owned on the porch one day
In years to come, leave him to a friend's couch.

There was only neon sizzling on and off on East 6th,
A near-dead Russian in another room, just feet away,
Curry and tabla skittering up the landing,
And a glaze of sheet, like skin, between them.

Things We Lost in the Crash

The firemen, cops, and rescue squad
Are still running around, their wives
Watching the door so late wondering
About tonight. In my head,
I'm still fumbling for that ring—
All palms and knees to asphalt like someone
Blindsided, glasses on the ground.
Somewhere in the weeds and brambles,
Perhaps tousling like a wooden Boy Scout ship
In a stream is a left-footed sandal—
I won't get that back.
There's a set of amber and blue glass stems
Crunched under the back hatch.
And as the squad clips the roof, curls it back,
Cuts my seatbelt to pull me out like a mummy,
A brittle thing, hitting air and light, a mist of rain,
For the first time, I look over, passenger,
Expecting you—there's no sound, no music—
The radio's busted. I can't find my watch.
There's no sudden rush or bustle, not you,
Just a seat, the shape of you nowhere to be found.

Waking a Sleeping Limb

She understands you can't poke
Such a thing and whisper—
There's no ear to yell into or kiss.
It flops in the negative
Space of her body's curve while a glass
From last night loses its fizz.
The arm lays there like fog covering
A city park bench and slide.
She must wait, crouched
In the rushes of midnight,
Patient as a sniper, or better yet,
Like the man at the bar who hasn't taken
A woman home in a long time—
A man who loathes his computer
For its dog-like companionship.
She rolls to her back, lifts
The limb with her good arm
And places it across her chest, then,
For a moment, holds the dead hand,
And it feels like another's hand
That has reached out to pay her
Some endearment or respect.
The lights of a city bus moan
On her ceiling, and just then,
The way an idea snakes into the mind
Or a visitor enters an empty room
And soaks into the emptiness,
Waits to fill the emptiness
With creak, voice or song,
There's a pin-prick at her pointer,
An ant stops cold on her outside palm.
She clenches a fist
And muscle memory returns.

The arm lifts and curls
The way it has before—
Remembering:
Wrapped around another
Or standing arm-in-arm,
That cold thing, the limb
Like a man catching fire.

Apology to My Buick Skylark

Your door locks punched
With screwdriver and knife,
During the divorce you sat
For a year, nearly stolen
A dozen times in the night.

I played chicken with you,
Said if they gave me you,
I'd take you to a field
And watch you burn—I never meant that.

Every minute you weathered
In my old drive,
I thought of changing your plugs,
Of the sound of hard rain off your hood,
Your 350's coughing, then solid start.

And with all paperwork signed,
Accounts settled,
The tow truck driver
Didn't charge me a dime

To drop you on the street
In front of my new place,
Under the crepe myrtle.
He cautioned me on firing you up
Too soon after such a time.

But when the offers came,
I let you go to make ends meet—(it was easy).
I watched your gold skin glint
Toward the stoplight at the corner.

Moving ever distant, you drove off—
Your trunk packed with the wild beast
Of my past kicking and howling
To get back here,
As if I owned it, as if it belonged to me.

Love and the Moon

Her breath changed as she looked over the craters.
A bead of sweat hit her lip—I saw it through her helmet's shield
As she stood beside the first print ever on the moon and flag
That said people like us had been here, but not us. Mons Agnes,
Lacus Deloris, Terra Vitae—as we passed all the sights,
We imagined the Dark Side with its endless night
And how lovers, eschewing morning, must have willed
It always just near dawn. Looking out, a cloudless night
And happy to be touring, we, our own postcard,
Beamed pictures home. With every bump and nudge
Of the lunar plain her hand tightened around my inner thigh.
She asked, what would *it* be like at zero gravity, I mean,
If we could slip off our suits, the hundred layers
Of space-age fiber between us, if I could touch
You like I want to, if only through this quarter inch
Of glass our lips could tease the softness of immortality
Out of the other, in this place with no season, no breeze,
Where we'll never feel not feeling it at all.

Man, one evening

Followed his wife
As she left to visit a sick friend,
Only she stopped off at a park,
Cut her lights and a shadow entered her
Car through the passenger's door.
The man was intrigued—
A sense of calm filled him the way
A child's body fills a small bed.
He watched as the figure wrapped
Its arm around the woman, his wife.
He was pleased by how reckless the hand
Ran the length of her cheek.
He imagined the conversation
They must be having
About how peaceful she was in the shadow's
Grip, how like herself she felt
For the first time in a while—
Even she felt like the cliché with which she swelled.
She must have mentioned
Her sick friend and how her husband
Would dial the phone after noticing
She was late, that her friend would answer—
It's my fault. I kept her over. She just left.
The shadow must know of their lives—
The way they pitched and yawed like rafts,
How he was a dog chasing sticks.
He waited a while, afraid to switch on his car,
But still he flicked a pebble in his giddiness
At the trunk of the woman's car. From where
He stood beside a dogwood,
He watched the rock flicker
Like the head of a match or the start
Of apology in the streetlight.
The man saw his wife's taillights flare
After the shadow exited the car.

The man was thankful
For the possibility that hit him,
Not like finding a road sign and arrow
After miles of wrong turns
In the high desert, the city up ahead,
Thousands there lost in the piñon pine,
Painted rock, and jack rabbit's eye,
But more like the surprise
Of strolling into a seedy bar
And finding himself
Sitting there at a vinyl booth
Like it was the front seat of a Buick,
His father beside him whistling Brubeck,
Missing the melody and head,
Him sitting there, pinned by the lights,
And flickering with booze.

Dead Boy

I knew nothing about stars,
Only that my mother was Gemini
Or Capricorn. I was Aquarius, born
In some year of the dog,
Yet I told him a week before school ended:
Your lifeline's short—look at your palm.
I'd heard it on a psychic hotline infomercial.

As we played it through, my bandanna cinched
Around my head like a madam,
A crowd leaned in to see how it all went.
What's it like for me—you know—
His curiosity like one tilting
Over the lip of a cliff.
I couldn't muster words
Like *riches, harem, lottery, fame*;
Only *crash, hay field, railroad—*
Your dead face for the senior class.

This is the last thing I'll say
About that boy who was—who curled
His Honda XR into a turn,
Rote as a handshake,
The early evening, a blank page:
He'd jeered, tripped
My friend in the lunch line.
He was not my friend.
He was the most earnest
On my father's ball team,
Nose like a scarecrow, bug-eyed,
Arms splayed
For a pop fly, left field,
The goddamned ball dropping
Like a word tripping off the tongue.

Man, one day, started believing

That when he was alone, he wasn't. He was sure
This was not a metaphorical haunting like those guys
With a dead wife whose presence is in every room
And everything the woman ever touched, including
The man's own body. This spirit-thing in his house
Was troubling, since he'd lost his faith years ago,
Was free of superstition, having snuck
God out of his house—tricked him into a bag,
And drove as fast as he could, at least a hundred miles
To a truck stop and left him there, thinking that if anyone
Needed God, it would be truckers, that God would
Hitch to a big rig and ride cross-country, happy to be
On the road like old times, performing miracles,
If only the simplest, like when he catches a lonely trucker
Staring into his empty glass, lamenting how fast
The whiskey goes, then upon looking away, and back
He finds his glass full again—God's favorite—
The miracle of the whiskey.
So this man was conflicted. He'd hear a knock
At the door, open it, and no one there. He'd go to the closet,
Pull out a jacket and his new roomie would suggest without words,
But it's colder out than you think, try this one.
Sometimes he'd want tea, and he'd walk to the kitchen
And there was his cup steaming on the counter.
What a life, he thought, to be haunted by a butler God
Or housewife God who brought his slippers
To his bedside during the night. The man was glad
And looked back over his life at the good
He must have done to receive these gifts,
Which he needed in his old age.
He got up in the morning to his waiting slippers,
Went to the kitchen for his waiting tea, then to his bed
For his waiting clothes, until, one day—nothing.
His slippers were where he left them by the bath,
Teabags tucked in the cabinet, no whistling pot,

His sweaters and pants lay on the laundry floor.
Many days passed. The house was a palpable emptiness.
The man grew old and hunchbacked.
He took to wearing a hat like old men wear and not leaving
The house. *What must I have done to deserve this.*
He remembered the God he took off all those years ago,
A quiet God, he left at a truck stop miles away
To fend for himself. How he must have felt, that God,
Left at a crossroads by a friend
And the man understood, he believed.

Teeth

There's a guy in Florida who took out
His own back teeth—*to slow the tremors,*
The ache from some fuzzy constellation
Behind my ear, he said. He put a little something on
The radio, a dance tune, throbbing
Like heartbeat, jabbed the pliers
In his mouth. Imagine that crack
When his hand seized, clamped to fist
And one tooth gave way,
Then another came after the cold steel
Slipped twice, snapped shut and bit his tongue,
Almost pissed himself.
Imagine his mother at the door,
Come down the hall smelling cigarettes,
Ice licking her top lip as she swigged,
The blaring drum and bass from his room
Thumping her back to the kitchen,
While the pliers went on with their hungry work.
And across the street is a party, an anniversary—
Feast and cake, dancing
Which he watched until the last
Headlights glanced his window,
The last light in the house burst into dark—
The last light in the Milky Way
Going out just like that.

Notes for a Wedding Toast:

The past is a cavalcade of bicycle bells behind you

Like a dress flapping around a lover's thighs

When your fingers were matchsticks lighting your way

Someone said, *The beautiful changes*

And yet the divine(r) is a peeper around corners

God of the near-empty cup

An urban explorer without a map of the trains

There will be empty rooms filled with people you know

And all they can say is *hello* and stare

And yet you raise your glass, you drink

Man once stood on his dock—

A small dock at the edge of a large lake
That trimmed his land to the dorsal shape of a shark
If viewed from a low-flying plane.
The man followed the line of houses across
The lake to where the horizon met an island
Or more aptly, a hill topped with pines,
In the center of the lake—
A place where high school kids
On weekends headed after slipping
Their parents' canoes into the water
Sprayed gold by sodium lamps,
And went to the island talking of archetype and Jung,
Or Odysseus and Troy, it makes no difference.
The man went to light his charcoal grill,
Saw his wife shape in the kitchen window,
Washing potatoes for dinner.
He splashed a cup of gas on the coals,
Stepped back, tossed a match, then walked the path
To the dock which creaked under his weight.
He took a cigarette from a pack in his jacket,
Lit that, watched the island,
Which did not move—capped with green,
Red dirt flowing into water
And saw a silver flash, perhaps a canoe, and again,
A silver flash, then again, and he understood—
Three short, three long, three short flashes and again—
And thought a couple kids, perhaps one of his own,
Out there, stuck on the island after a day flunking
A math final, then paddling out to the island
For sloppy sex and a good heart-to-heart
About being misunderstood.
He looked back at his wife in the kitchen window,
Could see her lips moving, singing, *Go get them.*
He checked the fire, which was beginning
To burn on its own—the coals just now glowing,

And he estimated he had time to kick
Off his shoes, strip to his shorts, leave his cell phone
On the lounger, dive, come up for air,
Count, like in college, count his strokes, pause
To mark the flash which was still flashing,
Three short, three long, then nothing,
And he imagined himself swimming
For the green-capped island,
His wife out on the dock now, calling
The neighbors who all come out
To watch the rescue of the kids
Who just went out to fool
Around and got into trouble.
There was a helicopter overhead making waves, news
Crews arriving from nearby cities and setting up
On his deck, awaiting his return,
The moment when he emerges from the water,
Exhausted, towel wrapped around his shoulders,
Mic at his lips, medics guiding him
To the gurney, oxygen mask strapped to his face
To soothe his cramps, the neighbors
Out waiting to lift him up
And shoulder a parade through their streets,
Him back with a story, one so heavy,
He could barely swim
Under its weight, how he saw the flash,
Jumped in, swam, followed the flash, until it sank,
How the kids went out to the red dirt island
To fool around, signaled
Him from a distance, how he swam,
Oh, how he swam
And barely made it back.

Cornered Beasts

The altercation begins with the attacker's
Head low and back,
The goal: always to keep the horns
Pointed toward the other,
To catch the opposition off-guard.
Both male and female mountain sheep,
Otherwise known as rams, are suited
Near equally for brawling, with the skull
Thick from territorial fights,
Neck muscles sufficient for locking horns
With no danger of injury, but that to ego, pride.
The fight may cease at any time, given
That escalation from the aggressor ends—
One need only back down or submit
To demonstrate any perceived aggression
Was only meant as play.
There is always the chance that a truce
Cannot be agreed upon and in such case
Each having displayed their weaponry
And knowing what's defended is worth the defense
Will try best to attack from the flank,
Horns ripping into his opponent,
Ripping organ, tearing muscle,
And breaking bone until the other falls,
Lays back in the grass and is down, left as food
For hunting carnivores or taken by the elements,
Bones left to one day intrigue a passing hiker.

The Spiders in My House

—For Kate Johnson

The spiders in my house wear bells—
Little ones so I know when they are near.
Newborns pour out a carol from the chimney.

Black widows and wolfs clang
From the toes of my shoes in the closet,
Kindly letting me know the danger they intend me.

They are soft with fur and some have claws.
They are cats, and we are birds in the yard—
My wife and daughter and me.

Their every step polites, *Next, please,*
As we move from room to room.
At night, their tiny lights bead from under the fridge

Or a cabinet's corner as I reach in for a mug,
Testing their hunger and resolve—
Their contentment with bellyfuls of fly and moth,

Proving that our truce is a golden mean.
I nap, they range and bring music
From the windowsill, picturing

Our bodies caught in silk—
Empty vessels to be filled.

Goners

On the day of my father's birth,
My father's father stood in the waiting room
In his khakis and boots, hands in his pockets
And watched a woman slam
Her purse in her car door and walk away,
Not knowing until the strap, growing taut,
Jerked from her hand.
At that point, he was exactly
Four years, eight months, three days and random hours
From the moment of his passing:
He'd slug out of Tuscaloosa General,
His appendix taken from his side,
And drive his '34 Studebaker toward home,
Fall asleep at the wheel
From medication and corn whiskey
And drift headlong into a logging truck.
The hospital oatmeal he took with him
Spilled on his smock and drooling down his leg—Goner.

May 1940, three years, six months, and some days
After Grandpa Virgil Jackson's end,
Hitler's boys crossed France
In their starched coats and boots, leaving
A long avenue of Goners—
My father, six at the time,
Still a citizen of rural Alabama, USA.

And it was about that time, only days apart,
That a family man in Bessemer, a neighbor, slid
From his horse, cigared, turned to his wife, two kids,
Did you see that? and was caught by a hoof to the gut—
Man down—a typical scene those days.
He soared into sleep, breathing, yet soon, a Goner.
The horse was put down—it too, a Goner.

All Goners, like scattered seed. And further on,
Grandpa Virgil, fourteen years gone now,
A luminary clock counting down,
My own father, though not a Goner to this day,
Ships out to Korea. He's seventeen,
Gunning down a beach of skins—
Eyes he cannot see, riddled in dark,
Imagining Alabama all around him:
An owl's call, July fly,
But the Black Warrior 7300 miles away,
A beach of Goners drifts before him.
In his mind there's kudzu sulking up the ridge,
Luke the Drifter on the radio,
The gray light of the drive-in falling on strangers,
Arm in arm, kissing, hands exploring
Where they have no business,
In a field, flung far, and lousy with Goners.

Nudiustertian

Relating to the day before yesterday.
—From Latin, nudius tertius

Man looked out over the sea.
The azul sway of sud and surf
Rocked like a machine gun squad. The palms
Were cooks pacing in a diner.
There was a fire down the beach
Where someone had just slit a pig's throat
To bleed it out before spitting.
There was a couple on a palapa,
And she felt pretty. Despite all that,
Despite mention of rickshaw
Or dinner, he couldn't help
But try to think of a word
He learned in school for the time
Before all happened and was left to silence;
He watched the surf beyond
The parasails and jet ski
Or kayak and skiff. He watched
The surf for a 100-foot water wall,
A cliff rolling at him, the moment
When he opens his mouth
And all that comes to him,
All he hears is a roar,
A chug, his voice yelling back
At him—his shorts yanked to his ankles
And he's back on the playground,
Beside the slide and seesaw,
His mates snickering, pointing,
A water balloon slapping him on the cheek.

In a Better Place

Without toothbrush and change of clothes in backpack,
So many have gone there—
Left just like that, given over to estate sale,
All their things: silver fork and spoon boxed up,
Jade dragon nested, and some young couple
Touring the living room discussing paint and furnishings,
Curtains with ruffle or not.
They are looking for their own better place,
Much like your father, though a shade now,
Who you imagine is waiting
With a whiskey and water to greet them on the porch—
He, no longer confusing
Night with brown sugar or parking tickets with hard rain.
We fall just like that—and boy, do we fall,
The bounced check of our youth still bouncing,
Its ping, ever-slight, and landing flat for a time.
Take your mother, two rooms over
For an entire childhood, flicking
A lighter, *Pick up your floor.*
And as you wait at the door for the couple,
To welcome them in, show them around,
It's like driving 500 miles to your bed,
With everyone in the car asleep,
The deer and mile markers shaving off the map.
You open the window, close it, open it again
To welcome the wet breath of night's empire in.
You blink for a moment too long,
Waking to your father shouting,
Look out, look out, look out—
His hands full of the same dark you let in.

Author's Notes:

"The light in bars, then, around the holidays": The line "what's the point of light/You have to strike a match to find?" is from Josh Ritter's song "Lantern."

Travis Denton lives in Atlanta where he is the Associate Director of Poetry@TECH and has served as McEver Chair in Poetry at Georgia Tech. He is also founding editor of the literary arts publication, *Terminus Magazine*. His poems have appeared in numerous journals, magazines and anthologies. *My Stunt Double* is his third collection of poems.

OTHER C&R PRESS TITLES

NONFICTION

Women in the Literary Landscape by Doris Weatherford, et al
Credo: An Anthology of Manifestos & Sourcebook for Creative
Writing by Rita Banerjee and Diana Norma Szokolyai

FICTION

Made by Mary by Laura Catherine Brown
Ivy vs. Dogg by Brian Leung
While You Were Gone by Sybil Baker
Cloud Diary by Steve Mitchell
Spectrum by Martin Ott
That Man in Our Lives by Xu Xi

SHORT FICTION

Notes From the Mother Tongue by An Tran
The Protester Has Been Released by Janet Sarbanes

ESSAY AND CREATIVE NONFICTION

Immigration Essays by Sybil Baker
Je suis l'autre: Essays and Interrogations by Kristina Marie Darling
Death of Art by Chris Campanioni

POETRY

Lessons in Camoflauge by Martin Ott
Dark Horse by Kristina Marie Darling
All My Heroes are Broke by Ariel Francisco
Holdfast by Christian Anton Gerard
Ex Domestica by E.G. Cunningham
Like Lesser Gods by Bruce McEver
Notes from the Negro Side of the Moon by Earl Braggs
Imagine Not Drowning by Kelli Allen
Notes to the Beloved by Michelle Bitting
Free Boat: Collected Lies and Love Poems by John Reed
Les Fauves by Barbara Crooker
Tall as You are Tall Between Them by Annie Christain
The Couple Who Fell to Earth by Michelle Bitting
Notes to the Beloved by Michelle Bitting

CHAPBOOKS

Paleotempestology by Bertha Crombet
White Boys from Hell by Jeffrey Skinner
Atypical Cells of Undetermined Significance by Brenna Womer
On Innacuracy by Joe Manning
Heredity and Other Inventions by Sharona Muir
Love Undefind by Jonathan Katz
Cunstruck by Kate Northrop
Ugly Love (Notes from the Negro Side Moon) by Earl Braggs
A Hunger Called Music: A Verse History in Black Music
by Meredith Nnoka

www.ingramcontent.com/pod-product-compliance
Lightning Source LLC
Chambersburg PA
CBHW031146090426
42738CB00008B/1235